Christianity

Anthony O'Hear and Judy Groves

Edited by Richard Appignanesi

ICON BOOKS UK   TOTEM BOOKS USA

This edition published in the UK in 2000 by Icon Books Ltd., Grange Road, Duxford, Cambridge CB2 4QF email: info@iconbooks.co.uk www.iconbooks.co.uk

Distributed in the UK, Europe, Canada, South Africa and Asia by the Penguin Group: Penguin Books Ltd., 27 Wrights Lane, London W8 5TZ

This edition published in Australia in 2000 by Allen & Unwin Pty. Ltd., PO Box 8500, 9 Atchison Street, St. Leonards NSW 2065

Previously published in the UK and Australia in 1993 under the title *Jesus for Beginners*

This edition published in the United States in 2001 by Totem Books

In the United States, distributed to the trade by National Book Network Inc., 4720 Boston Way, Lanham, Maryland 20706

Previously published in the United States in 1994 under the title *Introducing Jesus*

Library of Congress catalog card number applied for

ISBN 1 84046 166 7

Originating editor: Richard Appignanesi

Printed and bound in Australia
by McPherson's Printing Group, Victoria

Introducing Christianity

he

icene reed

I believe in one God the Father Almighty, Maker of heaven and earth, And of all things visible and invisible:

And in one Lord Jesus Christ, the only begotten Son of God, Begotten of His Father before all worlds, God of God, Light of Light, Very God of very God, Begotten, not made, Being of one substance with the Father, By Whom all things were made; Who for us men, and for our salvation came down from heaven, And was incarnate by the Holy Ghost of the Virgin Mary, And was made man. And was crucified also for us under Pontius Pilate. He suffered and was buried, And the third day He rose again according to the Scriptures, And ascended into heaven, And sitteth on the right hand of the Father. And He shall come again with glory to judge both the quick and the dead: Whose kingdom shall have no end.

And I believe in the Holy Ghost, the Lord and Giver of life, Who proceedeth from the Father and the Son, Who with the Father and Son together is worshipped and glorified, Who spake by the Prophets. And I believe in one Catholick and Apostolick Church. I acknowledge one Baptism for the remission of sins. And I look for the Resurrection of the dead, And the life of the World to come. Amen.

5

What is the Nicene Creed?

Orthodox Christianity has long been defined by the profession of faith, known as the Nicene Creed. Although named after the Council of Nicaea (a meeting of many bishops in what is now Iznik in Turkey in 325 AD), the Creed was not formulated there.

IT PROBABLY DATES FROM THE 5TH. CENTURY AD.

BUT IT DOES REFLECT THE DECISIONS OF THE COUNCIL.

The first Christian Roman Emperor Constantine (c. 280-337) called the Council of Nicaea.

IN ORDER TO STIFLE DISSENSION IN THE CHURCH.

The Council was pivotal in defining Christian belief about Jesus Christ and his divinity.

This Creed affirms that Jesus Christ is the only begotten Son of God, of one substance with God the Father, but that he was also a true man. Any account of Jesus has to consider both the life of the man Jesus, the historical person who lived in Galilee, and what Christians believe about him. Whether one is a Christian or not depends on whether one believes the Jesus of history is identical with the Christ of faith.

7

Jesus of Nazareth

The man whom we know as Jesus Christ was born during the reign of Augustus, the first Roman Emperor (63 BC-14 AD), around the year 4 BC. He was Jewish and brought up in Galilee, though he may not have been born there.

Wall painting found on a 1st century Roman catacomb.

COULD THIS BE THE EARLIEST PORTRAIT OF JESUS ?

During the final years of his short life, he became well known as a religious teacher in various parts of Galilee, Samaria and Judaea, including Jerusalem.

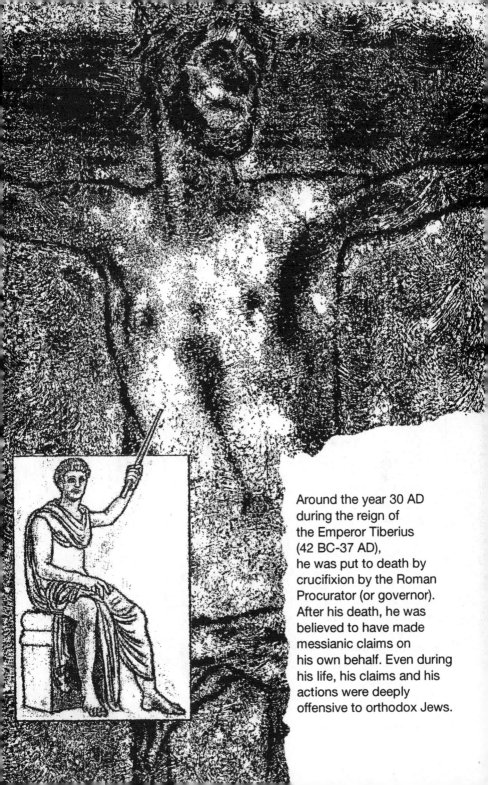

Around the year 30 AD during the reign of the Emperor Tiberius (42 BC-37 AD), he was put to death by crucifixion by the Roman Procurator (or governor). After his death, he was believed to have made messianic claims on his own behalf. Even during his life, his claims and his actions were deeply offensive to orthodox Jews.

The Evidence that Jesus Existed

After his death, his followers formed a sect, which has grown in strength ever since. They believe that Jesus rose from the dead, and that he is in fact God.

Within a century of his death, Jesus was mentioned as a real person by the Roman historians, Suetonius (c. 69-122 AD) and Tacitus (c. 56-117 AD), by the Jewish leader and writer Josephus (c. 37-97 AD), and also by the Roman writer and administrator, Pliny the Younger (c. 61-113 AD).

His followers also compiled various accounts of his life, known as gospels, from the Old English **godspel**, meaning good news.
Gospels attributed to the apostles of Jesus, **Mark, Matthew** and **Luke**, are widely held to date from 60 to 80 AD. A fourth, **John's** Gospel, was probably written after 100 AD.

Earlier than any of the Gospels were several of the numerous letters or Epistles of St. Paul.

THE EARLIEST IS MY FIRST EPISTLE TO THE THESSALONIANS OF ABOUT 50 AD.

There is also an early **Acts of the Apostles** which recounts the doings of the very early Church from Jesus' death until about 65 AD.

Jesus of History

All the early sources, Christian and non-Christian, take it for granted that Jesus was a real, historical person. An impartial and objective outline of Jesus' life, such as that given in the previous section, could have been written at almost any time since Jesus' death.

The Gospels provide fuller accounts, but these are strongly coloured by theological interpretations of Jesus' life and, in any case, were written a good 30 years or more after his death.

THIS DOESN'T MEAN WE SHOULD REJECT THEIR VALUE AS HISTORICAL SOURCES.

BUT IT DOES SUGGEST THAT WE CAN'T ALWAYS TAKE THEM AT FACE VALUE.

13

Chapter and Verse

In Matthew 24.30, Mark 13.26 and Luke 21.27, Jesus is represented as referring to a passage in the Old Testament Book of Daniel (chapter 7, verses 13-14): *I saw in the night visions, and, behold one like the Son of man came with the clouds of Heaven...And there was given him dominion, and glory, and a people.*

The reference is in Jesus' reply to his disciples on the Mount of Olives.

What shall be the sign of thy coming and of the end of the world?

...they shall see the Son of Man coming in the clouds of heaven with power and great glory.

Fact, Fiction or Drama Documentary?

Many New Testament scholars regard this and similar passages as words put into Jesus' mouth by the evangelists after his death, rather in the manner of much contemporary popular biographical writing which veers towards the fictional.

Can any writer know what was said in private between Queen Elizabeth I and the Earl of Essex? Such biographical guesswork is an attempt, not necessarily misguided, to reconstruct and make sense of earlier events.

Judaism at the time of Jesus

Having originally been desert nomads and after many wanderings and vicissitudes, by about 1000 BC the Israelites under David had formed a single kingdom. This comprised Jerusalem and most of the surrounding area on both sides of the Jordan, south to the Red Sea, and north into what is now Syria.

THIS IS THE FULFILMENT OF THE PROMISE OF A NEW LAND GIVEN BY GOD TO MOSES.

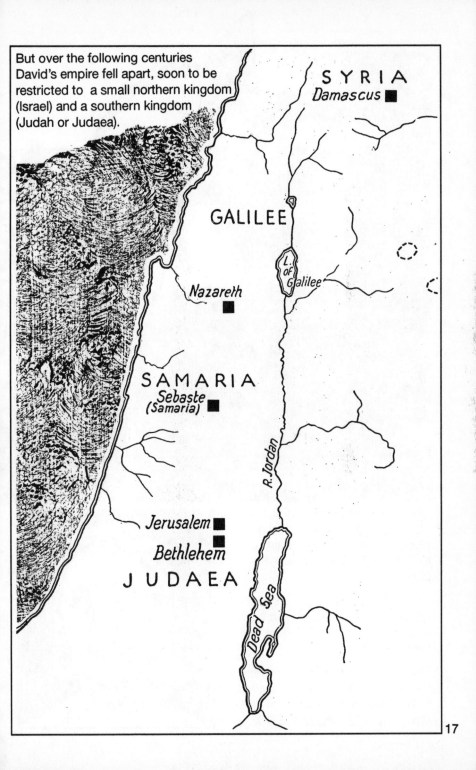

But over the following centuries
David's empire fell apart, soon to be
restricted to a small northern kingdom
(Israel) and a southern kingdom
(Judah or Judaea).

SYRIA
Damascus ■

GALILEE

Nazareth ■

L.
of
Galilee

SAMARIA
Sebaste
(Samaria) ■

R. Jordan

Jerusalem ■
Bethlehem ■
JUDAEA

Dead Sea

Israel fell to Assyria in 721 BC.
What was left of Judah perished
when Jerusalem fell and many of
the Jews were taken to Babylon in
587 BC.

A partial return to Jerusalem and
restoration of the Jewish cult there
was effected in 538 BC under the
then dominant Persians.

The area succumbed to Alexander
the Great in 333 BC and was ruled
by his Greek successors until the
Maccabean uprising of 165 BC.

The Jews then recovered a measure of independence, but internal strife brought about the effective annexation of Judaea by the Romans in 64-63 BC.

AT FIRST WE WORKED THROUGH LOCAL KINGS, LIKE HEROD THE GREAT.

I BEGAN A MASSIVE REBUILDING OF THE TEMPLE OF JERUSALEM.

Herod (73-4 BC) was half Arab, and only a Jew insofar as he was also half Idumean. The Idumeans had been forcibly converted to Judaism a generation or two before his birth.

19

Herod's reign represented a period of comparative peace and prosperity for his Jewish subjects, despite the numerous murders with which it was marked.

THE MASSACRE OF THE INNOCENTS AT THE TIME OF JESUS' BIRTH MAY JUST BE A STORY...

BUT IT'S QUITE IN KEEPING WITH HEROD'S CHARACTER!

Wearied with the problems of the area, in 6 AD the Romans installed their own man as Procurator of Judaea, though Herod's son Herod Antipas (21 BC-39 AD) remained ruler of Galilee.

TENSIONS BETWEEN THE JEWS AND US MOUNTED...

AND LED TO OUR CATASTROPHIC REVOLT AND ITS SEQUEL...

THE DESTRUCTION OF THE TEMPLE BY THE ROMANS IN 70 AD.

By this time, there were already four or five times as many Jews outside Palestine as in. (The so-called dispersion or **diaspora**.)

Old Testament Judaism

The most striking feature of the Old Testament is its relentless monotheism. The Israelites were distinguished from their neighbours in this respect.

OUR 2000-YEAR STRUGGLE UP TO THE TIME OF JESUS WASN'T JUST FOR LAND...

BUT IN LATER CENTURIES ESPECIALLY, EVEN MORE FOR PURITY OF FAITH IN THE ONE SINGLE GOD!

The Jews were constantly berated in the name of God by their religious leaders and prophets for anything which smacked of compromise with the world around them.

...they that forsake the Lord shall be consumed! (Isaiah 1.28)

It was their belief in their divine election which made them a particular threat to Roman sovereignty in Palestine, occasioning several disturbances even before 70 AD.

In Galilee itself, where Jesus was growing up, one such uprising ended in the crucifixion of 2,000 Jews.

Anyone appearing to challenge Roman sovereignty in the name of Judaism was an immediate danger to himself and, by virtue of possible reprisals, to the Jewish people as a whole.

I WAS BORN INTO A WORLD OF POLITICAL TENSIONS.

A Messiah for the Rebels

Throughout their history, the faith of the Israelites had a supernatural as well as a natural dimension. By the time of Jesus, many Jews hoped that God would send them a military Messiah, a new David to re-establish the kingdom by orthodox military means.

AND WE ZEALOTS BEGAN GUERRILLA ACTIVITY TO PREPARE FOR THIS!

A Messiah for the World's End

BUT SOME OF US BELIEVE THAT GOD'S KINGDOM WILL APPEAR ONLY WITH THE ENDING OF THE EXISTING WORLD ORDER.

WE AWAIT SOME SORT OF FINAL, APOCALYPTIC CATASTROPHE!

On this view, which doubtless owed something to Jewish military failures over the centuries, purity of heart and faithfulness to the Jewish law and tradition were means of preparing for the end which was nigh, in which righteous Jews would be swept into God's new kingdom.

27

Pharisees and Sadducees

There were many branches of Judaism at the time of Jesus, and Judaism was not a clearly defined phenomenon. Many strict Jews, for example, refused to recognize the Idumean Herod as a proper Jew. Diaspora Jews were often open-minded and cosmopolitan, even universalist in comparison to Judaic Jews, who tended to be fundamentalist and nationalist.

WE PHARISEES WERE THE LEADING GROUP OF JEWISH RELIGIOUS TEACHERS AT THE TIME OF THIS UPSTART, JESUS.

OUR TEACHING REPRESENTS THE BELIEFS AND PRACTICES OF A MAJORITY OF JEWS

WE INTERPRET THE LAW CAREFULLY AND IN A REASONABLE WAY.

WE BELIEVE IN LIFE AFTER DEATH, THE PUNISHMENT OF SINS – AND WE'RE ANTI-ROMAN!

The name Pharisee means that they were 'separated' or 'set apart'. This was understood to mean that they set themselves apart from those who would compromise with the heathens.

28

The Sadducees, by contrast, were the priestly caste. Their name derives from that of Zadok, the high priest of David. They were inflexible and impractical in their interpretation of the law.

The Essenes

The Essenes were an influential, relatively numerous and fanatical Jewish sect, not untypical of the time, who took the belief in the forthcoming apocalypse very seriously. Some time in the 2nd century BC they set up their own alternative to the Jerusalem Temple, a monastery at Qumran, near the Dead Sea.

WE WITHDREW FROM THE WORLD TO THE DESERT AND SET UP RULE-GOVERNED COMMUNITIES THERE.

THIS MAKES US PRECURSORS OF THE CHRISTIAN MONKS WHO UNDERTOOK A SIMILAR QUEST FOR SPIRITUAL PURITY IN THE DESERT FROM THE 4TH CENTURY AD ONWARDS.

Scrolls from Qumran monastery found in 1947 have had a startling effect on New Testament studies.

WE BELIEVE THAT JEWISH PRACTICE HAS BECOME CORRUPT AND NEEDS RENEWAL.

THE MESSIAH, THE TEACHER OF RIGHTEOUSNESS, WILL SOON COME TO DIVIDE THE WORLD INTO ELECT AND DAMNED!

EACH ESSENE COMMUNITY IS A TEMPLE, SPIRITUALLY SPEAKING.

Essenes made considerable play of ritual washing and communal meals. In some way their teachings, as manifested in the Dead Sea Scrolls, anticipate those of Jesus, just as their communal life foreshadows Christian monasticism.

Was Jesus an Essene?

The Essenes' apocalyptic writings were also marked by a militaristic violence, and even more, an exclusivity quite foreign to Christianity, if not to Jesus himself.

The extremism and apocalyptic fervour of John the Baptist, the latter-day Jewish prophet and Jesus' precursor, makes him look like an Essene, as Josephus suggests.

REPENT YE,
FOR THE KINGDOM
OF HEAVEN
IS AT HAND!

But John was closer to Jesus in anticipating the salvation of the whole Jewish people - and he wasn't militaristic.

And Jesus, though echoing some Essene themes, was no Essene. In his attitude to the law, he was closer to the Pharisees than to the narrow and bigoted Essenes, and certainly more humane.

The Wisdom of the Greeks

In the 5th century BC, the Chorus in Sophocles' **Antigone** speaks of man as the masterpiece of creation.

*...provident for all
(Not beaten by disease),
All but death, and death -
He never cures.*

Cure for death in the ancient world was often sought in the mystery religions such as the cult of Demeter at Eleusis, or the increasingly popular rites connected with deities such as Orpheus, Cybele and Mithras.

ORPHEUS

CYBELE

MITHRAS

In these rites, the believer 'died' with the god, a death often marked with a rite of purification, through immersion in blood.

New Gods, New Philosophies

The public, civic religions of Greece and Rome had, by the time of Jesus, largely given way to these cults of individual salvation on the one hand, and on the other, to systems of philosophy which stressed the desirability of individual contentment against a problematic universe common to all men.

OUR PHILOSOPHIES OFFER SOMETHING LESS EXOTIC, FRENZIED AND BLOODY THAN THE SALVATION RITES.

BUT THEY SHARE IN THE EMPHASIS ON THE INDIVIDUAL'S SELF-DEVELOPMENT AGAINST THE BACKGROUND OF THE UNIVERSE.

Stoics, Cynics and Epicureans all taught the need for the cultivation of calm rationality and peace of mind against the impulses and distractions of appetite, sensuality and public life.

EPICUREANS BELIEVE NEITHER IN GOD NOR GODS.

STOICS BELIEVE IN A GOD AS A WORLD SOUL, INMANENT IN THINGS AND IN HUMAN SPIRIT.

A WORLD SOUL THAT ORGANIZES THE UNIVERSE ON RATIONAL PRINCIPLES AND WHICH WILL ABSORB THE INDIVIDUAL AT DEATH.

By contrast again, Neo-Platonists, following Plato himself (c. 428-347 BC) in **The Timaeus** and **The Republic,** stressed the transcendence of God.

λογος

מִלָּה

THE WORD.

A DEMIURGE — A DIVINE **LOGOS** OR WORD — STANDS BETWEEN THE ULTIMATE DIVINE POWER AND THE WORLD IT CREATED.

Philo of Alexandria (c. 20 BC-c. 50 AD) is notable for managing to combine Neo-Platonic speculation with orthodox Judaism, although in his writings, as in those of many Neo-Platonists, the precise relationship between the Logos and the ultimate Godhead is far from clear.

PLATO IS BELIEVED TO HAVE HAD A MIRACULOUS BIRTH.

THE PHILOSOPHER AND MATHEMATICIAN **PYTHAGORAS** (C. 580 - 500 BC) IS SAID TO BE THE SON OF THE GOD HERMES.

ALEXANDER THE GREAT (350-323 BC) THE SON OF ZEUS AMMON, WAS DEIFIED IN HIS OWN LIFETIME.

IN 30 BC, THE POET HORACE ADDRESSED EMPEROR **AUGUSTUS** AS THE GOD MERCURY.

By the time of Jesus, straightforward belief in the gods of Olympus had been displaced by new philosophies and mystery cults, often of an Eastern provenance, and all sorts of quasi-superstitious beliefs about gods and men had wide currency. It was commonplace to think of great men as having semi-divine parentage.

Later Roman Emperors were routinely deified - which was the root of the problems that early Christians had with the Romans.

Gods appeared in human form from time to time, while even in Jewish circles it was believed that Moses, Enoch and Elijah had escaped death and gone straight to heaven.

The currency of stories and beliefs implying rather fluid distinctions between Gods and humans does not in itself show that we should discount the claim made by the early Christians about the divinity of Jesus, nor that in a Jewish context the claim would be regarded as other than startling. But they do point to the fact that minds in antiquity were, in general, more prepared to consider claims of this sort than we would be, were they made of a contemporary of ours.

The time of Jesus was one in which the divinization of the human was quite common. More importantly it was a time ripe for a religion able to combine the promise of individual salvation for each person with a monotheistic, philosophically plausible account of the cosmos.

MAYBE SO, BUT IT DOESN'T ENTIRELY EXPLAIN A MYSTERY.

WHY DID CHRISTIANITY— EMERGING FROM A BACKWARD AND PARTICULARIST JUDAEAN JEWISH CULTURE—BECOME SO UNIVERSAL AS TO ENGULF AND LONG OUTLIVE THE ROMAN EMPIRE ITSELF?

But we preach Christ crucified, unto the Jews a stumbling-block, and unto the Greeks foolishness.

St. Paul in his first Epistle to the **Corinthians** (1.23).

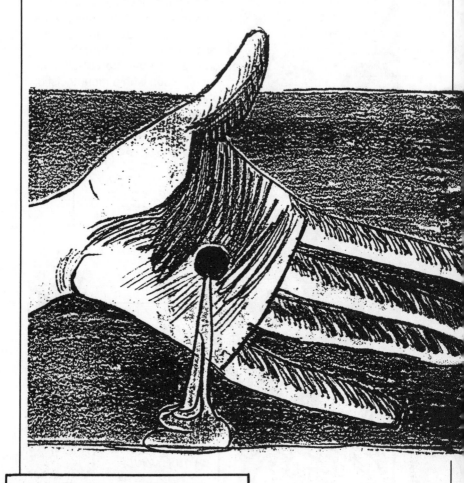

Preaching Foolishness?

FOOLISH, BECAUSE CRUCIFIXION IS A PARTICULARLY UNPLEASANT FORM OF EXECUTION RESERVED FOR NON-ROMAN CRIMINALS.

TRUE ENOUGH— BUT WHAT'S THIS "FOOLISH" TEACHING OF JESUS?

IS IT THE SAME AS ST PAUL'S WHO PREACHES "CHRIST CRUCIFIED"?

The Quest for the Historical Jesus

In the 19th century no less than 60,000 'lives of Jesus' were published. Here are two influential examples.

The **Essence of Christianity** (1900) by the German theologian Adolf von Harnack (1851-1930).

The **Life of Jesus** (1863) by the French historian Ernest Renan (1823-93).

Many of these 'lives', including some of the most famous, now seem dated, tendentious and anachronistic attempts to paint a picture of an ethical preacher enunciating the commonplaces of 19th-century liberalism and humanism.

In 1906, Albert Schweitzer produced his dissenting masterpiece, **The Quest of the Historical Jesus.**

Albert Schweitzer (1875-1965), German theologian, Bach scholar and organist, became a missionary doctor in 1913, establishing a hospital and leper colony in the wilderness of Gabon in Equatorial Africa.

I WAS EASILY ABLE TO SHOW THAT JESUS IS NOT THE 'GENTLE GALILEAN' IMAGINED BY RENAN AND MANY OTHERS.

And yet, Schweitzer's own conclusion - that who or what Jesus was is forever unknown, an 'ineffable mystery' - is itself melodramatic and uncalled for.

Even less justified is the lesson many have drawn from the failure of the 19th-century quest: that **any** quest for the historical Jesus can produce only a reflection of the times and the mentality of the quester.

1. Examination of the Gospels in the light of what we know of contemporary Judaism does allow us to draw a tolerably clear picture of the Jesus perceived by his earliest followers.

2. Given that many of these early followers actually **knew** Jesus, it is unlikely that this perception bears no relation to the underlying historical reality (Jesus himself).

3. Sketching a reasonably accurate picture of the historical Jesus is important, given that the central claim of Christianity is that in the person of Jesus, God has intervened finally and decisively in human history.

THAT SICKLY SENTIMENTAL JESUS WAS THE TARGET OF MY CONTEMPT!

German philosopher Friedrich Nietzsche (1844-1900).

The Gospel Accounts

Matthew attempts to establish Jesus' royal lineage by virtue of genealogy stretching back to King David and Abraham. This, and the accounts of Jesus' birth and childhood in Matthew and Luke, are regarded as highly questionable by many Biblical scholars today.

The star over Bethlehem at the birth of Jesus is also introduced as a miraculous proof of his origin, befitting a Son of God.

47

There are other differences, some of significance, between the four Gospels. They nevertheless agree in broad outline on the salient features of the career of Jesus. All four Gospels preface their accounts of Jesus' ministry with the prophetic figure of John the Baptist in the Judaean wilderness.

But when he saw many of the Pharisees and the Sadducees come to his baptism, he said unto them...

Jesus comes to John to receive baptism, and John recognizes him as the one who is to come.

O generation of vipers, who hath warned you to flee from the wrath to come?

...mightier than I, whose shoes I am not worthy to bear.

His ministry, lasting two or three years, is marked by a number of miracles and by forceful preaching, often in parables.

The blind receive their sight, and the lame walk, the lepers are cleansed, and the deaf hear, the dead are raised up, and the poor have the gospel preached to them.

Perhaps significantly, most of this preaching is in the country rather than in towns, where the Romans and established Judaism would have been more likely to take notice, and object. The fact that Jesus comes from Galilee may also be significant, as Galilee was a notorious source of political trouble for the Romans.

Some of Jesus' teaching involves wrangles with the Pharisees and other authorities.

Although popular with many of his hearers, Jesus is clearly a figure of controversy and a focus of dissent from orthodoxy.

Some of his preaching is private, even secret, addressed to a small band of chosen disciples.

Woe unto you, scribes and Pharisees, hypocrites! for ye are like unto whited sepulchres...

He that loseth his life for my sake shall find it.

51

The ministry ends with the death of Jesus in Jerusalem following a final and initially triumphant visit to that city at Passover time (a politically sensitive time when Jerusalem would have been packed with pilgrims celebrating the Jewish exodus from Egypt).

The last week of Jesus' life is treated in all the Gospels in far more detail than any other part of his life, emphasizing the centrality of his passion and death to the early Christians.

Jesus enters Jerusalem riding on a colt.

Jesus drives
the buyers and sellers
from the Temple.

He curses a barren fig tree -
and it withers away.

*My house shall
be called the
house of prayer;
but ye have
made it a den
of thieves.*

He disputes with the Pharisees and Sadducees - and prophesies the destruction of the Temple.

The Last Supper

As tensions increase, Jesus takes a ritual Passover meal with his apostles and teaches at length.

After a night
of agonized prayer
in the garden at Gethsemane,
Jesus is arrested,
having been betrayed
by his own apostle, Judas,
and disowned by another,
Peter.

He is taken
before the chief priests who
convict him of blasphemy.

The precise nature of the offence and blasphemy is not made entirely clear in the Gospel accounts, and has occasioned endless subsequent controversy.

Jesus offers neither resistance nor defence. He is scourged, crowned with thorns, and led outside the city to crucifixion on Mount Calvary.

Jesus dies on the cross and is buried. On the third day of his entombment, some women come to anoint the body, but find the tomb empty, with an angel at its entrance.

He is
not here;
for he is risen,
as he said.

Jesus then appears
to them - and to other
disciples on a number
of occasions - finally instructing
them to preach the 'good news'
to all nations.

Lo, I am
with you
always, even unto
the end of
the world.

For many in the 18th and 19th centuries - and even more in ours - the Gospel miracles present a profound problem.

Unfortunately for those embarrassed by the miracles, it is impossible to extract a miracle-free account of Jesus' ministry from the Gospels. Much of the preaching takes specific miracles as its starting point. The miracles are also presented as inspiring faith in Jesus in many witnesses.

What did Jesus preach?

If we extract the moral message of the Gospels from the surrounding narrative, much of Jesus' teaching does not seem especially revolutionary.

HARDLY SURPRISING AFTER 2,000 YEARS' EXPOSURE TO CHRISTIAN TEACHING IN OUR CULTURE!

BUT THE CORE ETHICAL VIRTUES WHICH JESUS PREACHED — WERE THESE REVOLUTIONARY IN HIS DAY?

Purity of heart, humility, love of one's neighbour, unaggressiveness, even to enemies, acknowledgement of the unimportance and corrupting effect of wealth and success, the 'golden rule' of doing as you would be done by.

More to the point, very little of Jesus' moral teaching would have been unrecognizable or unacceptable to pious Jews of his generation.

*Think not that I am come to destroy the law, or the prophets; I am not come to destroy but to fulfil...Till heaven and earth pass, one jot or tittle shall in no wise pass from the law, till all be fulfilled.***(Matthew** *5.17-18)*

AND THAT'S RIGHT IN THE MIDDLE OF THE SERMON ON THE MOUNT- HIS MOST COMPLETE MORAL DISCOURSE.

Jesus never said that the righteousness of the Scribes and the Pharisees is unnecessary, but rather that on its own it is incomplete.

Was Jesus Un-Jewish?

Jesus is represented in the Gospels as constantly tangling with the Pharisees, particularly over the interpretation of the law. In one incident, he is reproached for allowing his followers to pluck ears of corn on the Sabbath.

THIS IS EQUIVALENT TO WORKING ON THE SABBATH, AND IS THEREFORE UNLAWFUL.

Have ye never read what David did, when he had need, and was an hungred, he and they that were with him?
(Mark 2.25)

Jesus answers his critics by appealing to other scriptural instances which support (or seem to support) his position.

Jesus (in Mark, anyway, though not in Luke or Matthew who also recount the incident) goes on to say: *The sabbath was made for man, and not man for the sabbath.* **(Mark** 2.27)

THIS IS EVIDENCE THAT JESUS TOTALLY REPUDIATED THE SABBATH AND THE LAW, AND SHOWS HOW UN-JEWISH, EVEN ANTINOMIAN, HE IS.

German philosopher, G.W.F. Hegel (1770-1831), in **The Spirit of Christianity,** typifies many other commentators on this passage.

But this is almost certainly wrong. The Rabbi Simeon ben Menasya said something very similar to the words of Mark, in connection with the believer's duty to save a man's life on the Sabbath.

PROFANE FOR HIS SAKE ONE SABBATH, THAT HE MIGHT KEEP MANY SABBATHS.

In the light of the other things he said and did, it is doubtful that Jesus meant more than Simeon did - that there are sometimes duties to God and man which transcend those of a given stated law.

Nor is it the case that Jesus' preparedness to reason about the interpretation of the Law in the light of specific circumstances mark him off from the Pharisees and other orthodox Jews. Throughout Jewish history, in Jesus' time as much as now, there have always been reforming Jews, prepared to apply the Law in a sensible and reasonably humane way. Indeed, seriousness regarding the Law - which was supposed to characterize Pharisaism - demands no less. In attempting on occasion to question the literal application of the Law, Jesus can be seen as close to the Pharisaic tradition represented famously by his slightly older near contemporary, the Rabbi Hillel the Elder, who was widely recognized to be the greatest Jewish teacher of his time.

A Teaching for the End of the World?

By our current liberal ethical standards, the teaching of Jesus does not always seem in the least 'reasonable'. Consider some of his sayings.

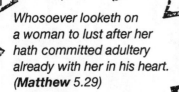

*Whosoever looketh on a woman to lust after her hath committed adultery already with her in his heart. (**Matthew** 5.29)*

(This **must** be an exaggeration!)

*It is easier for a camel to go through the eye of a needle, than for a rich man to enter the Kingdom of God. (**Mark** 10.25)*

(And, despite the efforts of medieval commentators to water this down, the needle through which the camel has to go was **not** a gate in the wall of Jerusalem. There was no gate of that name.)

That ye resist not evil: but whosoever shall smite thee on thy right cheek, turn to him the other also.
(**Matthew** *6.39*)

(This is a passage which has inspired countless professions of pacifism, including the great novelist Leo Tolstoy (1828-1910) and **his** disciple the Indian reformer Mahatma Gandhi (1869-1948), however futile a doctrine in dealing with really ruthless oppression.)

Take therefore no thought for the morrow: for the morrow shall take thought for the things of itself.
(**Matthew** *6.34*)

This, surely, is the most 'unreasonable', 'unrealistic' injunction of all, and one to which a religion and a body of churches lasting nearly two millennia can hardly have been faithful consistently. Indeed, this and kindred statements provide evidence to show that Jesus (or the Gospel writers at least) were expecting the end of the world **soon**, and that Jesus could not have been intending to found a religion lasting 2,000 years or more.
The unrealistic nature of these and other Gospel sayings poses problems for those who would follow the Gospels. Are these sayings to be regarded as colourful rhetorical exaggerations of standard and reasonably applicable virtues (chastity, indifference to worldly wealth, unaggressiveness, an acceptance of fate and suspension of desire)? Are they what they seem, fanatical injunctions to be applied fanatically? Or are they - as Schweitzer and others have contended - statements made by a man expecting the end of the world in a short time and not looking to enunciate principles for the general conduct of human affairs?

What did Jesus really mean?

Any serious reader of the Gospels, whether Christian or not, must come to some sort of decision about the **interpretation** of Jesus' teaching. Unfortunately the Gospels themselves do not give a clear answer. Jesus takes for granted the basic prescriptions of the Jewish Old Testament. Speaking to the rich young man who would follow him, he says:

Why callest thou me good?
There is none good but one, that is, God.
Thou knowest the commandments,
Do not commit adultery, Do not kill,
Do not bear false witness, Defraud not,
Honour thy father and mother.
(Mark 10.18-19)

BUT I'VE DONE ALL THAT...

One thing thou lackest:
go thy way, sell
whatsoever thou hast,
and give to the poor,
and thou shalt have
treasure in heaven:
and come, take up
the cross, and
follow me.
(Mark 10.21)

Even this apparently clear directive is hard to interpret.

DOES IT APPLY TO **ALL** CHRISTIANS — OR ONLY TO SOME CHOSEN ONES?

IN ANY CASE, WHAT DOES FOLLOWING JESUS MEAN?

While the familiar parables and sayings of the Gospels certainly indicate watchfulness before God, generosity of spirit, repentance, humility - they remain parables and sayings.

THEY DON'T AMOUNT TO A CODE OR SET OF COMMANDMENTS.

69

In the Gospels we are confronted with Jesus as a **leader**, a person who speaks and acts with authority, and who demands a decision. And here he is quite different from the Pharisees and un-Jewish. Where Jewish commentators appeal to their sources in the Old Testament, Jesus speaks on his own behalf.

Even the great prophets of the Old Testament, such as Isaiah and Jeremiah, report what the Lord says. Jesus speaks in his own voice, prompting the observation from soldiers sent by the priests and Pharisees to arrest him that....

Never man spake like this man.
(John 7.46)

Jesus' manner of speaking is surely the root of his blasphemy, for it implies that he is putting himself on a level with God. It has correctly been said that the central message of the Gospels is not the teaching of Jesus, but Jesus himself.

Jesus and the Kingdom of God

> **But I tell you of a truth, there be some standing here, which shall not taste of death, till they see the kingdom of God.**
> *(Luke* 9.27)

MEANING...
THE END OF THE WORLD
MUST BE NEAR!

Whatever we make in detail of Jesus' precepts, it is clear from the Gospels that we are not to act in a humble or charitable or a peaceful way because these are the humanitarian things to do. The Gospels, like the Essene writings and like John the Baptist's teaching, are infused with great urgency about the coming of the Kingdom of God. The Kingdom of God will be brought about by divine action, following a bitter battle with the forces of evil. Men have a consequent and urgent need to repent and reform.

*If any man will come after me, let him deny himself, and take up his cross daily, and follow me...Whosoever shall be ashamed of me and my words, of him shall the Son of man be ashamed, when he shall come in his own glory, and in his Father's, and of the holy angels. (**Luke** 9.23-24)*

Theologians and New Testament scholars can argue endlessly about the authenticity of speeches such as these.

It is surely significant that the prophetic verse from Luke (9.27) is also found in Matthew and Mark. So, even if Jesus himself did not believe in the imminence of the Kingdom of God, many of the early Christians did. Sections of the early Church, then, if not Jesus himself, appear to have been **mistaken** on a major issue of fact!

Even if he did not believe in its imminence, Jesus certainly preached the Kingdom of God and told his followers to preach it too as a matter of urgency. Some theologians have argued that the Kingdom is a quasi-ethical state which Jesus' work has already in some sense initiated, at least among his followers, even before the end of the world. It cannot be said that this interpretation fits well with the passage we have been looking at, or with Jesus' threat to the unrighteous.

There shall be weeping and gnashing of teeth, when ye shall see Abraham, and Isaac and Jacob, and all the prophets, in the kingdom of God, and you yourselves thrust out.
(Luke 13.28)

When the son of man shall come in his glory, and all the holy angels with him, then shall he sit upon the throne of his glory. And before him shall be gathered all the nations: and he shall separate them one from another, as a shepherd divideth his sheep from the goats.
(Matthew *25.31-2)*

Jesus, as 'Son of Man', then will come to judge the whole world. While the Kingdom certainly has an ethical, spiritual dimension - and while Jesus' followers can anticipate the Kingdom in their own lives - it clearly also had a **cosmic** significance for Jesus and the evangelists.

Even more alarming to the modern mind is the suggestion that the Kingdom may be primarily or even exclusively intended for the Jews.

I am not sent but unto the lost sheep of the house of Israel. **(Matthew** 15.24)

This is the reply of Jesus to a Gentile woman seeking his aid (**Matthew** 15.21-28). 'Lord, help me,' she insists, and Jesus answers roughly.

It is not meet to take the children's bread, and to cast it to the dogs.

Truth, Lord: Yet the dogs eat of the crumbs which fall from their master's table.

Oh woman, great is thy faith: be it unto thee even as thou wilt.

Jesus seems only to concede that the 'dogs under the table' (the Gentiles) may eat 'the crumbs of the children's bread' (what is **left over** from the Jews' salvation).

This passage, also found in Mark (7.24-30), leans towards the exclusivity and severity of the Essenes.

There is no doubt that for Jesus his mission is first and foremost to the Jews, and only secondarily and as a side-effect to the Gentiles. As we shall see, though, narrow nationalism of this sort is overturned most notably in Paul, but also in John (10.16) in the Parable of the Good Shepherd where Jesus speaks of laying down his life for his sheep, including sheep *'which are not of his fold'*. Had it not been overturned there would, of course, have been no chance of Christianity becoming a world religion.

Jesus, the Anointed

Are we then to look at the man Jesus as essentially **a** or **the** Jewish Messiah? Strictly and linguistically, Messiah = Christ = anointed: so Jesus Christ = Jesus Messiah. Everything hangs on what we, or the Jews or Jesus himself, mean by 'Messiah' beyond 'anointed'.

Luke (7.37-50) tells of a repentant woman sinner, who comes to wash Jesus' feet with tears, wipe them with her hair, kiss them and anoint them with oil.

Thy sins are forgiven.

Who is this that forgiveth sins also?

This episode suggests the anointing of a king - and possibly a super-human one.

The Messiah, the Son of Man, the Son of God

For the Jews, the ritual anointing of a king with oil was a sign of God's choice of that king. By the time of Jesus, the title of Messiah had come to be applied to the future individual who would initiate God's kingdom. Some Jews anticipated an ordinary human leader, but others who saw the kingdom in apocalyptic terms expected the Messiah to be sent from heaven, from a previous existence by the side of God. This figure was known by the title customarily rendered in English as 'the Son of Man'.

This title is used by Jesus in the Gospels over sixty times, far more often than that of Messiah, to which Jesus answers directly and unambiguously only in Mark's account of his trial.

It is indeed striking that throughout the Gospels, Jesus renounces direct political ambitions. It is not just that his kingdom is not of this world, but more that the kingdom he is interested in will bring about the end of all earthly kingdoms, probably in the not too distant future.

79

The Kingdom of the Poor?

Consistent with this unworldliness is the continual suggestion in the Gospels that the kingdom Jesus is preaching is one for the lowly and the poor and the outcast, as much as for the rich and powerful.

At the same time, the joy and hope and inclusiveness of the Gospels does not preclude violence and judgment towards those who choose not to be numbered with the son of peace.

I tell you, Nay: but except ye repent, ye shall all likewise perish.
(Luke 13.5)

NOT EXACTLY A PEACEFUL MESSAGE!

And the constant attacks Jesus makes on the Pharisees and the lawyers, drawing attention to their hypocrisies and cruelties towards their fellow men, leave little doubt as to their eventual fate.

If Jesus rejects political Messiahship, the Gospels do on many occasions present him as the Son of God. In his baptism by John, he saw:
the Spirit like a dove descending upon him. And there came a voice from heaven, saying Thou are my beloved Son, in whom I am well pleased. (**Mark** 9.7)

Devils who are exorcised cry before him:
Thou art the Son of God. (**Mark** 3.11)

And throughout John's Gospel, Jesus in his discourses identifies God as his Father.
But we cannot conclude from this and other references in the Gospels that Jesus saw himself as the Son of God in the precise sense given to that phrase by the Nicene Creed. For one thing, the phrase 'Son of God' as used at the time had a variety of meanings in addition to the literal one: faithful Jew, great man, special representative of God, perhaps even Messiah. For another, we cannot be sure that the Gospel writers did not interpolate the phrase themselves into the key passages at some date after Jesus' death. Nor indeed can we be entirely sure that when Jesus uses the phrase 'Son of Man' he is always using it to refer to himself, or that it always bears the sense of demi-god or more.

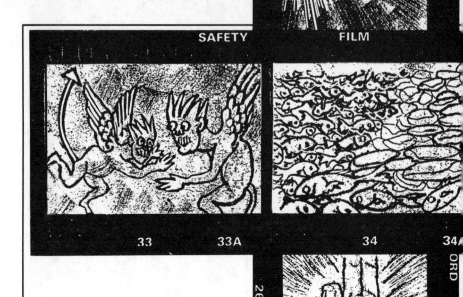

Nevertheless it would be extraordinary if the Gospel picture of Jesus as a divine or semi-divine figure able to cast out devils, heal, raise from the dead, multiply loaves and fishes and quell storms, and sent to establish a new relationship between God and Israel at least - if this picture did not bear some relationship to the sorts of claims Jesus made on his own behalf.

We should remember that his first followers were pious Jews, to whom the claims being made would have seemed blasphemous had they not been given strong reason to believe them - and where better than from Jesus himself?

What would be extraordinary is not the falsity of the claims, but the supposition that people could believe such things of a man whom they knew and decided to follow unto death, and, at the same time, put such thoughts and words into his mouth if he himself had, while alive, given no inkling of any such interpretation of his life and work.

35A   36   36A

...all things are possible to him that believeth.

Lord, I believe; help thou mine unbelief.
(Mark 9.23-24)

For Jesus' contemporaries, including the Gospel writers, and arguably for Jesus himself, the plausibility of the claim to divinity would have been vastly enhanced by the miracles. And that Jesus had some extraordinary power of healing cannot be ruled out, even by rationalistic 20th century non-believers. It would, indeed, be all of a piece with the powerful, stormy and mysterious figure whose portrait emerges strongly from the Gospels.

85

The Cross

The strongest and perhaps only completely unambiguous lesson which emerges from the preaching is that men are called urgently to repent in the light of what is to come. Jesus' own claims and personality challenge us no less to make a decision, a decision made the more poignant by the fact of the Cross.

We preach Christ crucified.
(1 Corinthians 1.23)

The true subject of the Gospels, as indeed of Christianity itself, is not a teaching or a philosophy, but a **person**.

How did Jesus himself think of his own death? The Gospels are not always clear.

The Son of Man is delivered into the hands of men, and they shall kill him; and after that he is killed, he shall rise the third day.
(Mark 9.31)

But this and similar passages may be interpolations.

It is clear though, that Jesus did not resist his arrest or attempt to defend himself at his trial. It is also clear that the Jewish leaders were determined to rid themselves of him and ask the normally hated Romans to help them in doing this, though less clear exactly why this was or what the crime was for which he was condemned by them.

However, again in **Mark** (14.61-64) we are shown the High Priest questioning Jesus.

Art thou the Christ, the Son of the Blessed?

I am...

Then the high priest rent his clothes, and saith...

Ye have heard the blasphemy, what think ye?

*And they all condemned him to be guilty of death. (**Mark** 14.64)*

Ecce Homo (John 19.5)

The doctrine may not have been a total stumbling-block (**skandalon**, in Greek) to the Jews, who would have been familiar with the idea of a servant suffering vicariously for the people.

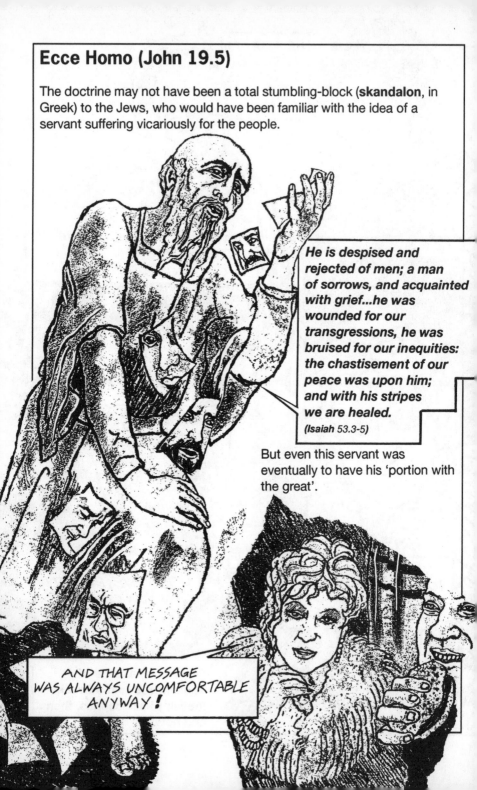

He is despised and rejected of men; a man of sorrows, and acquainted with grief...he was wounded for our transgressions, he was bruised for our inequities: the chastisement of our peace was upon him; and with his stripes we are healed.
(Isaiah 53.3-5)

But even this servant was eventually to have his 'portion with the great'.

AND THAT MESSAGE WAS ALWAYS UNCOMFORTABLE ANYWAY!

The Irony of the Cross

It is always easier to swallow a hard doctrine when it is sanctified by time and softened by familiarity. That this doubtless uncouth, troublesome and disturbing Jesus might be God's specially anointed, and that his message might involve so complete an abdication of worldly hope, would doubtless be too much for the great and the good of his (or any) time, particularly in view of the constant attacks Jesus makes on the great and the good. If, though, the Cross was the means by which the Jewish leaders hoped to stop the Jesus movement forever, by an irony cruel to the Jews, the cross turned out to be the matrix in which Christianity itself was formed. For the message that Jesus represented, crystallized in his death and resurrection.

The Resurrection

All the Gospels and all the early Christian writings witness to a belief in Jesus' physical resurrection from the dead. As Paul put it, with admirable directness:

If Christ be not risen, then is our preaching vain, and your faith is also vain.
Yea, and we are found false witnesses of God; because we have testified of God that he raised up Christ...And if Christ be not raised, your faith is in vain; ye are yet in your sins.
(1 Corinthians *15,14-15,17)*

The foolishness of the Cross is a temporary foolishness: one which is transformed and vindicated by Jesus' resurrection, which is itself a token of the eventual resurrection of those who die in Christ.

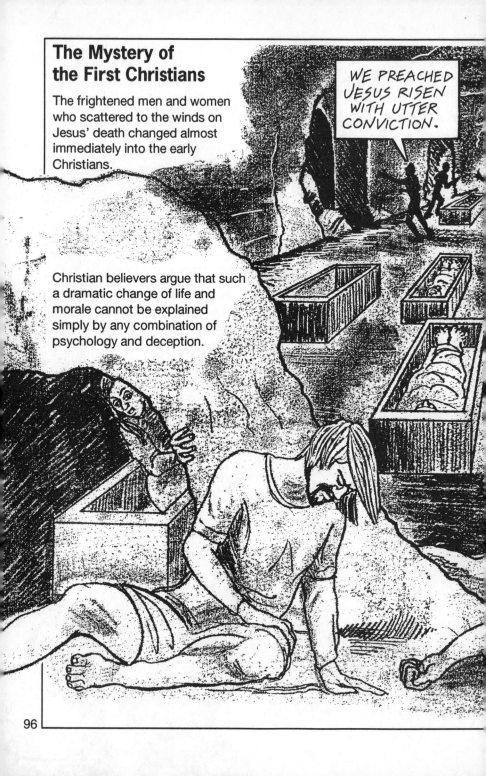

The Mystery of the First Christians

The frightened men and women who scattered to the winds on Jesus' death changed almost immediately into the early Christians.

WE PREACHED JESUS RISEN WITH UTTER CONVICTION.

Christian believers argue that such a dramatic change of life and morale cannot be explained simply by any combination of psychology and deception.

UNTIL MANY OF US TOO SUFFERED MARTYRDOM.

From our distance in time and mentality from 1st century Palestine, it is extremely difficult to be sure about what happened in the tomb and to the first Christians in the first days and weeks following Jesus' death. Even less is it easy to determine just what can be achieved by more or less conscious self-deception and wishful thinking. And while, when confronted with the testimony of believers to miraculous and spiritual experiences, the standard rationalistic explanations in terms of auto-suggestion seem altogether too glib, no assessment of the early days and subsequent success of Christianity can ignore the fact that in their own ways the rise and persistence of both Judaism and Islam are equally remarkable and equally 'miraculous'.

Nor can we overlook the fact that other stories of miraculous resurrections from the dead are by no means unknown in the ancient world. Even in the Gospels themselves there are at least two others (those of Lazarus and Jairus' daughter), and they are not presented as happenings of a type completely alien to the experience of those who witnessed them.

While travelling to Damascus to purify the synagogue of Christian elements, Saul receives a vision of Jesus.
(*Acts* 9.3-19).

Saul, Saul, why persecuteth thou me?

Who art thou, Lord?

He then becomes the Apostle Paul, an equally ardent and active follower of Christ. Persecution turns into conversion - a pattern of early Christianity.

The Birth of Christianity

If Jesus' message is hard to extract from the Gospels and from what we can discern from his own teaching, the Christian doctrine as represented by St Paul and the Acts of the Apostles is comparatively straightforward. In its straightforwardness, though, we lose sight of Jesus the man and his doings and sayings, and begin to focus on the Son of God, his atoning death and his resurrection and our participation in his saving act. The message of this Christianity, like that of the Gospels, concentrates on Jesus rather than on his teaching. Unlike the Gospels, however, Pauline and Apostolic teaching focuses hardly at all on Jesus' deeds or human personality. Or rather, it focuses on the ultimate non-deed of Jesus - his passion - and on its cosmic significance.

Paul is the first apostle not to have known Jesus in person. He is in this sense the archetype of the convert who bears witness to Jesus on the basis of **faith**.

Paul made converts throughout the Jewish diaspora, but also among non-Jews (Gentiles). In so doing, Paul transformed Christianity from a proclamation to the house of Israel into a universal religion, speaking to the whole world. He also spelled out the meaning (or a meaning) of Jesus being both *'Lord and Christ'*.

Pauline Christology

We may now speak of Christ and of Christology, as our subject matter is not so much Jesus the human person, as the anointed one of God, who turns out to be God. Christians believe that Jesus of Nazareth and the Son of God are two aspects of the one person. Christology (the study of Christ) is the attempt to explore the relationship of Christ to God, and for Christians merges into theology (the study of God).

Paul's Christology is the earliest and in many ways the clearest statement of Christianity. It certainly goes beyond anything Jesus taught, and not just because, compared to Jesus' teaching, it is systematic and comprehensive. For the early Christians, the fact that Paul and others developed and extended the teaching of Jesus was not necessarily objectionable, although Paul had to struggle to get his particular attitude to Jewish Law accepted in a Church which was initially Jewish. We must bear in mind that for them Jesus was alive, in contact with them, and, in all probability, soon to return from heaven *'with his mighty angels in flaming fire taking vengeance on them that know not God, and obey not the gospel of our Lord Jesus Christ'* (**2 Thessalonians** 1, 7-8).

According to Paul in *Galatians* 4, 4-7, the Gospel is **this:**

...when the fullness of time was come, God sent forth his Son, made of a woman, made under the law, To redeem them that were under the law, that we might receive the adoption of sons.
And because ye are sons, God hath sent forth the Spirit of his Son into your hearts, crying Abba, Father, Wherefore thou art no more a servant, but a son, and if a son, then an heir of God through Christ.

GOD'S SON WAS MADE OF A **WOMAN** – AND UNDER THE **LAW.**

BUT THIS DIDN'T MEAN THAT PAUL THOUGHT ONLY JEWS COULD BE SAVED.

It was on this point that Paul's argument with the Judaizing Christians centred. We have to remember here that Christianity began as a Jewish sect, preached by Jews to Jews initially in Judaea and seen by them as the culmination of the Jewish faith. Paul's perspective as a diaspora Jew was rather different from that of the disciples who had known Jesus, and this difference became accentuated when, in his work in the Jewish diaspora, he started making Gentile converts.

Jesus' redeeming death saves not just the Jews, but all mankind; and in this saving death, recognized as such by the resurrection, all are freed from the obligation to submit any longer to the detail of the Jewish law.

THE LAW HAD THE ROLE OF TUTOR OR GOVERNOR UNTIL THE APPOINTED TIME CAME FOR CHRIST'S SACRIFICE AND **ALL** OF US CEASED TO BE CHILDREN.

WE STILL HAVE TO OBEY THE COMMANDMENTS — BUT WE'RE FREE FROM THE LAW.

Indeed, over-concentration on the law and on works, which we find in Israel, suggests that salvation comes by our own efforts rather than by God's grace and favour. The Israelites *'stumbled at that stumblingstone'* (**Romans** 9.32), and failed to recognize both the limitations of the old law and its annulment, and the universal scope of God's gift.

105

Jewish Christianity vs. Universal Christianity

Needless to say, the radically un-Jewish slant of Paul's teaching was contested by many of his fellow Christians, but at the Council of Jerusalem (AD 49) Paul's view by and large prevailed. Christianity could and did now develop fast as a world religion, spreading through the Roman Empire, unshackled by its racial and legalistic origins.

It was also able to survive the fall of Jerusalem in 70 AD, and the destruction once more of Jewish hopes.

Did Jesus not say - *'I will destroy this temple that is made with human hands, and within three days I will build another made without hands.'*
Mark 14, 58.

Jesus, too, had insisted on a man's inner dispositions as being more important than outward observance of the Law, but if Matthew, Mark and Luke are to be believed, he can hardly have expected so complete a repudiation of the Law as we find in Paul. From Paul's point of view, the joyful message brought by Jesus is not just ultimate liberation from death and evil - though it is that - it is also freedom now from the crippling burden of Jewish law and observance.

Un-Jewish Greek ideas?

Could Jesus have seen himself as that for which the whole creation *'groaneth and travaileth'* following the sin of Adam, the first man, as Paul puts it at the beginning of his Gospel?

THESE NOTIONS OF JOHN AND PAUL ORIGINATE IN GREEK-BASED PHILOSOPHY.

LOGOS - THE PRIMEVAL EXPRESSION OF THE CREATIVE GROUND OF EVERYTHING, AND THAT WHICH ORGANIZES THINGS RATIONALLY.

But to suggest that, because ideas of John and Paul are Greek in origin, **therefore** they are notions necessarily foreign to Jesus is quite wrong. It suggests a far more rigid separation of Greek and Jewish ideas than there actually was in 1st century Palestine.

But is He Man or God?

The difficulty with Jesus seeing himself as the 'divine Word made flesh' is not that the notion of the divine Word could never have occurred to him. It is rather that a man who knows that he is God (and who presumably knew he would outlive his mortal life) would have so completely different an attitude to his suffering and death and to his life generally that it is doubtful that he could be regarded as a genuine 'man' at all.

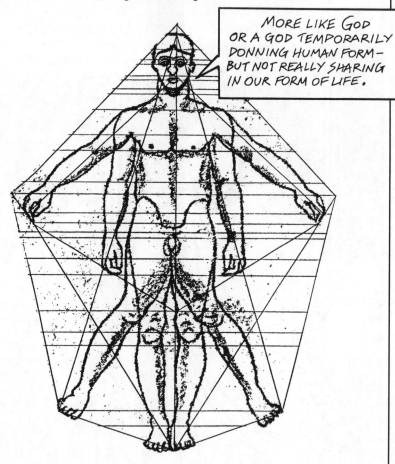

MORE LIKE GOD OR A GOD TEMPORARILY DONNING HUMAN FORM— BUT NOT REALLY SHARING IN OUR FORM OF LIFE.

On the other hand, it is hard to see how a God could temporarily suspend his divinity and all knowledge of it, and still in this new form **be** God! The story of Jesus in the Church is very much the story of oscillations between stress on Jesus the **man** and stress on Jesus as **God**.

The Immaterial Divine in Material Form

In the world influenced by Greek thought, there was constant speculation about ways in which the **immaterial** principle which governed all things manifested itself in **matter**.

Orthodoxy and Heresy: (1) Docetism

It is not surprising that with the spreading of Christianity into the non-Jewish world, and with the ever more forceful assertion of Jesus' divinity, attempts should be made to interpret Jesus' humanity as a **disguise** or semblance taken on by a purely divine being.

Docetism has been a constant theme in Christianity from the early days. It is often combined with a mistrust of the material aspects of our existence, a conviction that God could never have sunk himself into foul matter.

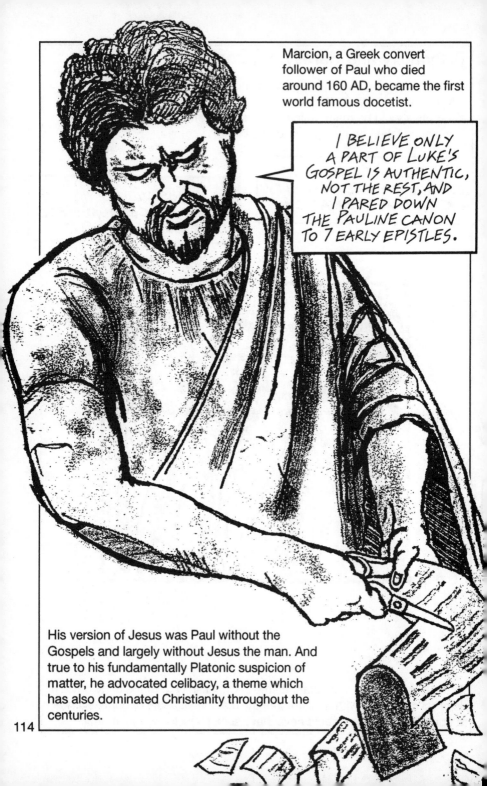

Marcion, a Greek convert follower of Paul who died around 160 AD, became the first world famous docetist.

I BELIEVE ONLY A PART OF LUKE'S GOSPEL IS AUTHENTIC, NOT THE REST, AND I PARED DOWN THE PAULINE CANON TO 7 EARLY EPISTLES.

His version of Jesus was Paul without the Gospels and largely without Jesus the man. And true to his fundamentally Platonic suspicion of matter, he advocated celibacy, a theme which has also dominated Christianity throughout the centuries.

Against the Flesh

Origen (c. 185-c. 254), one of the first great thinkers of the Church, castrated himself.

St. Augustine (364-430), perhaps second only to Paul as a theologian, wrote somewhat salaciously of 'down there'-

THAT PLACE FROM WHICH THE FIRST SIN IS PASSED ON.

THERE BE EUNUCHS WHICH HAVE MADE THEMSELVES EUNUCHS FOR THE KINGDOM OF HEAVEN'S SAKE.

And the early desert monks, from the 4th century on, engaged in prodigious feats of mortification to ward off fleshly temptation.

115

Jesus not anti-Sex

But in what we know of Jesus' own teaching, we can find little warrant for hatred of sexuality. The Jesus of the Gospels appears at ease in the company of women. He preaches the sanctity of marriage, and the possibility of his having been married cannot be completely ruled out.

Even Paul had to concede, in *Corinthians* 7, 9...

Arianism

Orthodoxy, even when Greek in inspiration, never accepted the implications of docetism - that Christ's body was some sort of illusion or phantasm, and his sufferings accordingly unreal.

BUT WE HAD A TREMENDOUS BATTLE WITH THE ARIANS' REFUSAL TO ACCEPT THE DUAL ASPECT OF JESUS FROM THE OPPOSITE POINT OF VIEW.

I, ARIUS, HOLD THAT JESUS WAS NOT FULLY AND ETERNALLY GOD!

This doctrine of Arius and his followers looked like capturing the Church in the early 4th century.

117

Christ's deification would therefore be like that of Greek mythic figures like Herakles and Ariadne - mortals raised to Olympus after particularly deserving lives.

NO, THAT'S NOT ACCEPTABLE.

The Council of Nicaea attempted to put Arianism down in the year 325 by asserting that Jesus was one in essence (consubstantial) with the Father, a position finessed in 451 at the Council of Chalcedon which asserted that Jesus had two natures in one person, and was fully man and fully God.

The Anthropic Principle

The Christological doctrines of Nicaea and Chalcedon are not easy to accept or even understand. Nevertheless, the idea that the ultimate principle (or **Logos**) of the universe could and did take on a particular and specific human nature without losing its divinity is a claim of astonishing boldness. It implies that human nature is an image of the cosmos itself, a thought which has received renewed currency recently in the **anthropic principle** of modern astrophysicists and cosmologists.

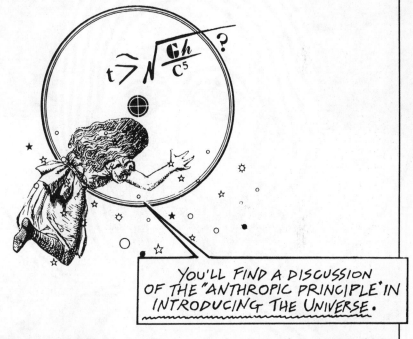

$$t > \sqrt{\frac{Gh}{c^5}} \; ?$$

YOU'LL FIND A DISCUSSION OF THE "ANTHROPIC PRINCIPLE" IN INTRODUCING THE UNIVERSE.

According to this principle, insofar as we are products of a universe which had its origin in an original 'Big Bang', the conditions necessary for our existence had to be **present** at the Big Bang. Some strong versions of the principle imply that human life and consciousness were in some rather obscure sense **intended** in the Big Bang. But the Christian idea that the Logos has been made flesh in Jesus goes way beyond even a strong version of the anthropic principle, when put in the context of the salvation story. *'The Word of God has become human so that you might learn from a human being how a human might become divine,'* as a favourite saying of the Greek fathers of the Church had it.

119

Jesus, the Pantokrator

The Jesus who is the Logos is the divine spark who restores the creation which, according to the myth, fell away through Adam's sin. He is the way, the light and the truth. He is also the ultimate judge and ruler of all.

The Pantokrator, 'all mighty', from the Greek **panto,** 'all', and **krator**, 'mighty', was depicted in the classic images (icons) of the Greek and Russian Orthodox Church.

And yet, in the icons of Christ the All Mighty, is there not a hint of docetism?
What has this vision of a transformed humanity to do with the man, Jesus of Nazareth? A concentration on the cosmic role attributed to Jesus is all too likely to distract attention from his earthly life.

From Early Church to Imperial Religion

Christianity had started as a Jewish heresy. Under the influence of Paul, it became a religion in its own right.

As already said, the time was ripe for a new religion which combined fervent spirituality with a promise of individual salvation and some hope of intellectual development. And the cosmopolitan and extensive Roman Empire was a perfect medium for its expansion.

EXCELLENT COMMUNICATION SYSTEMS — BY LAND AND SEA!

The Persecutions

Unfortunately, Christianity quickly came to be seen as subversive. As early as 52 AD, Christians were expelled from Rome by the Emperor Claudius (10 BC-54 AD). Paul himself was executed under Nero (37-68 AD).

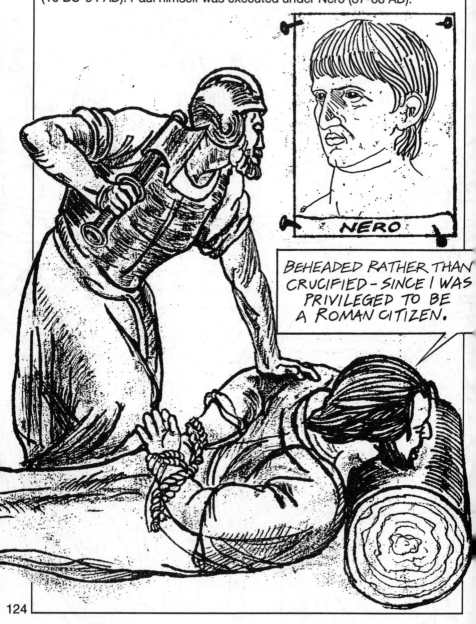

NERO

BEHEADED RATHER THAN CRUCIFIED - SINCE I WAS PRIVILEGED TO BE A ROMAN CITIZEN.

Further martyrdoms and sporadic persecutions of Christians followed, sometimes initiated in response to particular local crises in the Empire.

WE'RE ACCUSED OF ALL SORTS OF CRIMES...

INCEST, ORGIES AND CANNIBALISM...

Christianity's other-worldliness, its attraction to slaves, its tight communities clearly offended many.

125

'No to the Emperor!'

But the official point of crisis was the Christians' refusal to participate in Emperor worship, and this led to major and systematic persecution in the second half of the 2nd century. By the year 200, there were enough Christians in the Empire to **overthrow** it.

AND OUR MEMBERS WERE NOT CONFINED TO THE LOWER CLASSES.

THE CHURCH HAS BISHOPS AND A WIDE ADMINISTRATIVE STRUCTURE...

AS WELL AS BITTER AND VENOMOUS FEUDING OVER ORTHODOXY!

Confrontation with the Empire grew as the Church grew in power and influence. There were large-scale persecutions under the Emperor Decius and Valerian in the middle of the 3rd century, and again under the Emperors Diocletian, Maximian and Galerius in the early 4th century.

Constantine Christianizes the Roman Empire

By the time of the Emperor Constantine's capture of Rome in 312, the persecution of Christians had become not just wasteful of effort but counter-productive.

This was the policy Constantine adopted, although he also found it necessitated his imperial intervention in the Church's internal squabbling over doctrine (the Council of Nicaea).

Christianity thus became the official religion of the Roman Empire, both East and West, from that time on, saving only a rather futile effort on the part of Emperor Julian 'the Apostate' to restore paganism in his short reign (361-3).

JULIAN THE APOSTATE

Jesus the Man: Ruler or Slave, Suffering Servant or Political Liberator?

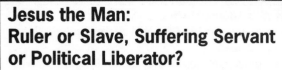

Once Christianity became the Imperial religion in the early 4th century, it was only natural that Jesus' role as ultimate ruler and judge of the universe should be emphasized, and that this should be reflected in the iconography. Constantine is said to have received a miraculous sign - and divine help - at the Battle of the Milvian Bridge in 312.

And it doubtless led to the thought that Jesus Christ, 'the All Mighty', could on occasion take up arms against his enemies.

Christianity as the established religion of the empire began to take on more of the properties of empire itself.

AFTER ALL DIDN'T JESUS HIMSELF SAY, 'I BRING THE SWORD'?

BISHOPRICS WERE PRIZES WORTH HAVING.

DUE TO THE DONATIONS OF THE FAITHFUL, THE CHURCH BECAME RICH.

CHURCH ZEALOTS PURSUED MISSIONARY AIMS MILITANTLY FAR AFIELD.

The State Religion of Christendom

By the end of the 6th century, when there was no emperor in Rome, the Bishop of Rome became recognized as head of the Church in the West, equal in power and influence to the surviving eastern Roman Emperor in Constantinople.

THE PATRIARCH IN CONSTANTINOPLE NEVER ENJOYED THE SAME POWER I HAD AS THE POPE IN ROME.

As a state religion and as a state in its own right at times, the Church has always been able to draw on the elements of kingdom and judgement of the Gospels. The conception of Jesus as ultimate ruler, which has often been used to uphold dynasties and crusades, tends to emphasize the **divinity** of Christ.

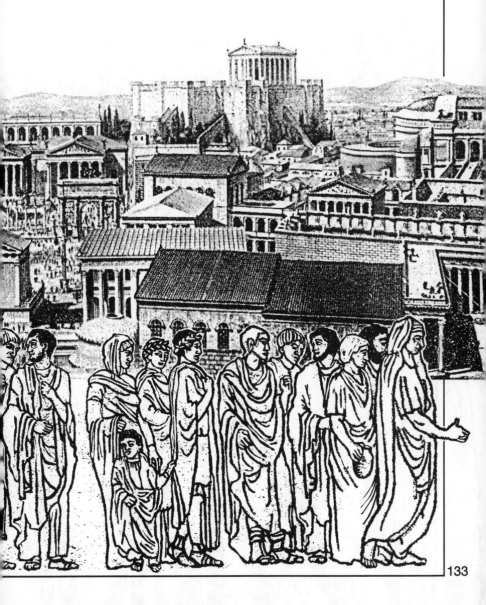

Following Jesus in Poverty

On the other hand, there have always been followers of the Gospels unhappy with worldly pomp, and unhappy with any attempt to associate Christianity with the world and its rulers.

In this, of course, they can point to many incidents in the Gospels, and in Jesus' own words as recorded in them. In addition to the story of the rich young man, and the saying about the camel and the eye of the needle, we have the words Jesus spoke in sending forth his disciples:

For Francis, as for Thomas à Kempis (c. 1380-1471), the author of **The Imitation of Christ**, Ignatius of Loyola (c. 1491-1556), a Spanish ex-soldier and mystic who founded the Jesuits, and many, many devout Christians from the Middle Ages on...

DEVOTION CONSISTED IN CONFORMING AS FAR AS POSSIBLE TO THE LIFE AND CHARACTER OF THE GOD-MAN JESUS.

Devotional Meditation

This imperative, accordingly, encouraged a concentration on the life of the man Jesus - or more accurately, to what assiduous **meditation** on the Gospels revealed of the man Jesus, not necessarily the same thing. In the case of Francis, imitation of Jesus went as far as the reception of the **stigmata**.

Meek and Mild as the Child Jesus

Franciscan devotion involved extremes of asceticism and bodily chastisement, in order to identify closely with Jesus' passion.

Although mistrust of the body and the search for mystical union with the divinity of Christ had always been themes in Christianity, in Francis and his followers these basically world-denying concerns were somewhat softened by a lively devotion to the humanity of Jesus, and particularly to his childhood.

It was Francis who was largely responsible for the medieval cult of the nativity, cribs, donkeys and all.

Unfortunately, as we have already noted, the Gospel accounts of Jesus' birth are now generally regarded as mythical. And more catastrophic to Francis' own mission to preach poverty and the Cross, before Francis himself died in his hermitage in 1226, his followers...

WITH THE MONEY LAVISHED ON US BY THE FAITHFUL WE'RE GOING TO BUILD THE GREAT BASILICA AT ASSISI!

Millenarianist Revolutionaries

At every stage of the history of Christianity, the austere and prophetic Jesus of the Gospels has to be reclaimed from the consequences of the worldly success of the preaching of that Gospel. Often the attempt to rescue the man Jesus, and what is taken to be his message, from the established Church order has gone along with a wild and lawless **millenarianism**.

MILLENNIUM = A PERIOD OF 1,000 YEARS...

AND A MILLENARIANIST BELIEVES IN CHRIST'S PROPHESIED REIGN *IN PERSON* ON EARTH!

Throughout the Middle Ages, there are examples of rabble-rousing attacks on established order of any sort.
In 1251, after the failure of the Fourth Crusade to do more than sack Christian Byzantium, an ex-monk called Jakob led a large army through the north of France.

So-called 'free spirits', believing themselves to be above morality, terrorized peaceful communities in the 14th century. In the 14th, 15th and 16th centuries, movements occur again and again preaching equality and anti-clericalism in the name of Jesus. There are indeed Gospel passages which seem to support extreme political positions.

Luther

At other times, renewal produced movements of genuine spiritual power, such as that of Francis himself, and of the reformer, Martin Luther (1483-1546).

Luther emerges in history first as a vitriolic critic of the wealth of the Papacy.

PARTICULARLY AGAINST THE TRAFFIC IN RELICS AND INDULGENCES, THE BASIS OF THE CHURCH'S IMMENSE WEALTH!

One effect of attacking the wealth and power of the Church is to leave the world to the secular power, something for which there is a famous Gospel precedent:

Render to Caesar the things that are Caesar's, and to God the things that are God's. (Mark 12,17)

SO DID JESUS ANSWER TO THE PHARISEES ABOUT THE LEGITIMACY OF PAYING TAX TO THE ROMANS.

Luther was quite happy with this consequence of his views, and opposed attempts to set up Christian politics on earth.

RIGHTLY SO, IF YOU LOOK AT THE TOTALITARIAN EXPERIMENTS OF MUNTZER AND CALVIN...

When the Saints come marchin' in...

Thomas Muntzer (c. 1490-1525) was a priest who preached class war and imminent apocalypse, leading to a revolt of the peasantry. He was executed a decade before followers took over the city of Munster.

They set up a messianic monarchy assisted by a committee of public safety.

The reformer John Calvin (1509-64) set up a theocracy in Geneva in the 1540s which was more benign, but only comparatively so. Pastors and disciplinary officials were supposed to enforce the moral code, visiting every house annually for the purpose. Opponents ('Libertines') were expelled and sometimes tortured and executed.

ADULTERERS ARE TO BE EXECUTED!

WE BEHEADED A YOUNG MAN FOR STRIKING HIS PARENTS!

Jesus, 'Our Contemporary'

Luther's underlying criticism of relics and indulgences, ideological rather than political, was an assertion of the Pauline doctrine that men are saved not by their own efforts, but by God's free gift.

SALVATION IS BY GOD'S GRACE ONLY...

At the same time, Luther had a lively sense of Jesus as a contemporary.

In common with most medieval artists and commentators, Luther made little effort to portray Jesus as a 1st century Jew.

IN MY SERMONS, JESUS IS VERY MUCH OUR CONTEMPORARY DEMANDING A CONTEMPORARY RESPONSE.

In this context, Luther's translations of the Gospels into strong and lively vernacular German were crucial.

CHRIST WAS ALSO A 15TH CENTURY GERMAN IN MY PAINTINGS TOO.

Albrecht Dürer
(1747-1528)

AND LUTHERANISM INSPIRED MY MUSIC.

J.S BACH
(1685-1750)

Loyola's Meditational Discipline

The Lutheran emphasis on the living, concrete reality of the Jesus of the Gospels was paralleled in the Catholic tradition by the **Spiritual Exercises** of Ignatius of Loyola, in which an equally concrete and equally anachronistic effort was made to bring the person of Jesus before the 16th century believer's imagination.

In the **Spiritual Exercises,** the 'excitant', like Ignatius himself, withdraws from everyday life for a month.

He then meditates on the Gospels, imagining himself to be present at the events of Jesus' life, death and resurrection.

... ASKING MYSELF — WHAT WOULD I HAVE DONE, HAD I BEEN PRESENT.

AD MAJOREM DEI GLORIAM

The culmination of the exercises is the 'election' at which the excitant decides to devote his life to following Jesus in a spirit of complete obedience and humility.

The Jesuits

Ignatius' exercises formed the basis of the order he founded - the **Society of Jesus** or **Jesuits**.

Other Catholic Mystics

At the same time in Catholicism, there were ever more ecstatic, if not fanciful attempts to enter into a mystical relationship with the figure of Jesus, conceived of as 'the bridegroom of the soul'. The Spanish mystic, St. John of the Cross (1542-91), speaks of the aim of spirituality as being the divine betrothal of the soul and the Son of God.

En una noche obscura
Con ansias en amores inflamada
o dichosa uentura
sali sin ser notada
Estando ya mi ... sose...

... segura
... calá disfraçada
... uentura
... y ençelada
... ni casa sosegada

... ueya.

... ardia

THE DARK NIGHT
Songs
of the soul, which rejoices at having reached
that lofty state of perfection:
union with God by the way
of spiritual negation

His fellow Carmelite and co-founder of the Discalced (or barefoot) branch of the order, St. Theresa of Avila (1515-82), experienced the mystical piercing of the heart by a spear of divine love en route to her mystical marriage with Jesus.

The English poet and Catholic mystic, Richard Crashaw (1613-49), like St. Theresa, writes of Christ's passion in ecstatic and highly sensuous tones.

STEPS TO THE TEMPLE

On the wounds of our crucified Lord.

O these wakeful wounds of thine!
Are they Mouths? or are they eyes?
Be they Mouths, or be they eyne,
Each bleeding part some one supplies.

Lo! a mouth, whose full-bloom'd lips
At too dear a rate are roses.
Lo! a bloodshot eye! that weeps
And many a cruel tear discloses.

O thou that on this foot hast laid
Many a kiss, and many a Tear,
Now thou shalt have all repaid,
Whatsoe'er thy charges were.

This foot hath got a Mouth and lips,
To pay the sweet sum of thy kisses:

Emphasizing the Person in Christian Mysticism

The Jesus with whom these Catholic mystics are in communion may be some distance from the historical person of Jesus, but he is in recognizable continuity with the subject of mysticism from the days of the early Christian desert hermits to St. Bernard of Cluny (fl. mid-12th century) and the early medieval monasteries.

Christian mysticism, however ecstatic and overpowering, always retains a connection - however tenuous - with the physical person of Jesus.

WITH JESUS AND THROUGH JESUS THE SOUL ACHIEVES UNION WITH GOD.

And this emphasis on **individuality** distinguishes Christianity from the all-engulfing Buddhist or pantheistic forms of mysticism.

...IN WHICH THE ADEPT LOSES HIS PERSONALITY AND SOUL IN A FORMLESS VOID.

The Sacred Heart of Christ the King

Devotion to a clearly largely fictitious and sentimentalized Jesus reached its apogee with the Catholic devotion to the Sacred Heart of Jesus. Latin and particularly South American Catholicism presents an unexpected transformation of the same figure as Christ the King.

The idea behind the Sacred Heart is that Jesus, though risen, is still suffering mentally if not physically, and is looking for consolation in the form of special prayers from the devout.

AND WE IN TURN WILL RECEIVE SPECIAL REWARDS FOR OUR DEVOTION.

Christ the King reveals that the Jesus of sentiment is also ruler of the world, though whether temporal or spiritual is not always entirely clear.

Liberation Theology

The concept of Christ the King has in recent years undergone a remarkable transformation, particularly in South America, being replaced by Christ the **liberator**. So-called 'liberation theologians', such as the Jesuit Jon Sobrino and the Franciscan Leonardo Boff, teach in a way rather like their medieval predecessors.

Liberation theologians can certainly point to scriptual passages which exalt the poor and the suffering, but whether Jesus ever intended (in Sobrino's words) that the poor should 'inaugurate God's kingdom' in a political sense, is another question altogether.

IT SHOULD PROMOTE POLITICAL LIBERATION AND ECONOMIC REFORM ALONG MARXIST LINES.

Far removed as these versions of Jesus are from the historical Jesus - as far removed in their way as is the liberal 'historical' Jesus of the 19th century - they do reveal both the enduring power of Jesus to inspire, and also his protean character, his ability to take on myriad shapes and representations.

Is there anything of the strange and impetuous figure of the New Testament in the Jesus of popular devotion? We may reject the suffering, sentimental and ultimately vengeful aspects of the figure projected as much by contemporary 'liberation theology' as by the Sacred Heart and Christ the King, but...

BUT... There is one respect in which every version of Jesus Christ which we have considered **is** united.

Even from the distance of two millennia, it is the uncomfortable, challenging person of Jesus, calling now for a radical reappraisal of my - and your - relationship to God and man which remains central to Christianity, rather than his multi-faceted and often ambiguous teaching.

Assenting to the Lord Jesus

Jesus commands assent from his followers, because for them he is the instrument of salvation. The man, Jesus of Nazareth, after his resurrection becomes the Lord Jesus Christ, crucified, risen and urging us on.
In Jesus, God, the Wholly Other, becomes man. In Jesus, the humanity of God is revealed.

Foolishness and Wisdom

'If the fool would persist in his folly, he would become wise.'
William Blake, from **Proverbs from Hell**, 1793.

This is a transformation of worldly wisdom, because from the wordly point of view Jesus is a **failure**, and in order to participate in his success, believers have to identify themselves with the Cross, and with Jesus' failure. Hence, in many of them, extremes of asceticism and world denial. And hence, too the continual tendency in the Church to renewal, to return to its unworldly origins from the wordly success, which its call for total commitment brings to the Church, time after time.

In Jesus and the Christian Churches condense a cluster of ideas of continual fascination and attractiveness and - for some - repulsiveness. There is the idea of the divine breaking into human life, and in so doing to repair the insufficiency of mankind, our mortality and weakness, and also the chaos of the cosmos.

167

The Idea of Redemption

There is the idea that our own weakness or suffering is or can be **redemptive**. There is the idea that God's best representation is a suffering man. These ideas suggest that the universal principle underlying the world as a whole **can** and **does have** a particular concrete manifestation.

THESE INFINITE SPACES TERRIFY ME...
Blaise Pascal (1623-62), theologian and mathematician
...ENDLESS TIME ENDLESSLY RECURRING...
Nietzsche was also fascinated and repelled by the idea of 'Eternal Recurrence'.
AN INFINITELY EMPTY COSMOS – THE ENDLESS INJUSTICES OF HISTORY... DOES ANYTHING HAVE A MEANING?

In Christianity and in Jesus, time and space are tamed and humanized. And perhaps only a religion that can accommodate the reality of a divine incarnation can assuage and justify the predicament of human suffering and mortality. Finally, the Christian idea that permits a radical re-thinking and re-doing of our conceptions of ourselves and our relationships offers us a restoration of personal integrity that we know we have lost.

THERE is not one Moral Virtue that Jesus Inculcated but Plato & Cicero did Inculcate before him; what then did Christ Inculcate? Forgiveness of Sins. This alone is the Gospel, & this is the Life & Immortality brought to light by Jesus, Even the Covenant of Jehovah, which is This: If you forgive one another your Trespasses, so shall Jehovah forgive you, That he himself may dwell among you; but if you Avenge, you Murder the Divine Image, & he cannot dwell among you; because you Murder him he arises again, & you deny that he is Arisen, & are blind to Spirit.

William Blake, from **The Everlasting Gospel**, 1818. 171

Can we 'explain away' Christianity?

The non-believer will explain the enduring success of the Christian religion by appealing to its doctrinal, institutional and emotional power, to its appearance at a propitious moment in history, and even more, to the power of the enigmatic and forceful personality of Jesus, and perhaps, too, to the continuing ability of Jesus to be all things to all men without disappearing entirely. On the other hand, for the non-believer the figure of Jesus of Nazareth is simply too slender a reed to bear the weight of interpretation and theology which his followers from Paul onwards have placed upon him.

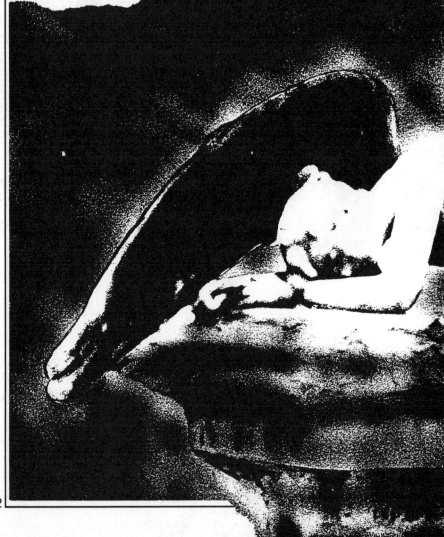

The non-believer may well be correct, but even if he is, he will have to admit to the centrality of Christianity's immense contribution to the development of European culture, art and thought and particularly to the humanitarian and universalist ideals it has bequeathed to the rest of the world. He will also have to explain how it is that Christianity and its ideals could prove so powerful as to make the time of Jesus, in retrospect, a turning point in world history - or, to put the point another way, to explain how it is that so powerful and endlessly fascinating a complex of ideas could condense on so unlikely a figure as Jesus of Nazareth, unless there was indeed something of super-human force about him.

Further Reading

In quoting the Bible I have used the King James or Authorized Version. Published first in 1611, the Authorized Version is neither the first nor the most accurate English translation. It may not even be the greatest, but it is certainly the most familiar, the most resonant, and one of the most endowed with meaning, flexibility and gravity. Even at the end of the 20th century, it is hard to see that it would present serious difficulties of understanding to speakers of English. For those who prefer more modern versions, there are many, including the New English Bible, the Jerusalem Bible and the Good News Bible, all of which have their supporters.

There are, of course, countless books purporting to be biographies or studies of Jesus himself. Many of them say as much about their authors as about Jesus. A short, up-to-date and well-balanced account is Humphrey Carpenter's **Jesus** (Oxford University Press, 1980), which includes pointers to reliable further reading on the subject.

A less direct, but probably more fruitful way of beginning to study the subject of Jesus and what he means is to survey the relevant historiography. Here I would particularly recommend **The Interpretation of the New Testament, 1861-1986**, by Stephen Neill and Tom Wright (Oxford University Press, 1988). All the influential writers on Jesus and the New Testament over the past couple of centuries are there, from Niebuhr and D.F.Strauss in the early 19th century, through to Harnack, Renan, Schweitzer, Bultmann, Barth and Dodd, up to the present.

All are put in their context, allowing the reader to come to a reasoned evaluation of what they say. Naturally, this would be impossible for someone who had read just one book, however good or famous, whether it was Renan's, say, or Schweitzer's, or A.N.Wilson's, or even this one. It is particularly important to remember the need to evaluate what one reads in this area, one in which nearly every view has, and can be shown to have, elements of tendentiousness.

On the Gospel texts themselves, the Penguin New Testament commentaries are very good: D.E.Nineham on **Mark**, G.D.Caird on **Luke**, John Marsh on **John**, and John Fenton on **Matthew**. Nineham's introduction to the **Mark** volume contains a judicious introduction to Jesus and the Gospels as a whole.

On the history of Christianity, there are again many, many books. Characteristically sweeping, comprehensive, learned and acerbic is Paul Johnson's one-volume **A History of Christianity** (Penguin, 1978), a good starting point for further investigation. On the interpretation of Jesus and images of Jesus over history, Jaroslav Pelikan's **Jesus Through the Centuries** (Yale University Press, 1985) is something of a pioneering work, taking the subject thematically. It is informed by considerable learning and a generous spirit.

All the books mentioned will send the interested reader in a host of different directions, and provide more or less adequate signposts for their journeys.

Acknowledgements

Thanks to **Oscar Zarate** for the illustrations on pages 15 and 164, and also for the hand lettering; and to **Willy Becherelli** for the angel on pages 172–173.

Thanks to the following people who posed for the drawings of some of the book's main characters: **Linda Knutson, Oscar Zarate, Howard Peters, David King, Amy Groves, Zack Wellin, Deane Waerea, Anthony Goldstone, Reuben Knutson, Anny Brackx, Mandy Learmonth**.

Typeset by **Marta Rodriguez**

Anthony O'Hear is Professor of Philosophy at Bradford University. He is the author of many books and articles on philosophy, including *Experience, Explanation and Faith: A Study in the Philosophy of Religion*.

Judy Groves is a painter, illustrator and designer. She has also illustrated *Philosophy, Wittgenstein, Lacan, Plato, Lévi-Strauss* and *Chomsky* in this series.

Index